ScrapMan

Carolyn Bear

Illustrated by John Prater

OXFORD
UNIVERSITY PRESS

Chapter One

Winston was the owner of a scrap-yard. People brought him broken gas cookers and bits of rusty iron and old worn-out cars. He had a machine that could crush a car until it was no larger than a TV set.

But before Winston crushed anything he would check to see if there were any bits worth keeping.

He had a big shed full of useful things that he had saved. The only problem was... what was he going to do with them?

Winston liked to go into his shed after work and potter about. He took things apart with his screwdriver and put the useful bits together with other useful bits from other things.

One night, he was trying to fix the good bits saved from a broken mobile phone into the working part of an old washing machine. Suddenly he noticed something. The way he had put them together looked just like a face... and this face seemed to be looking back at him.

That's how he first had the idea of making Scrapman.

Once he'd had the idea he couldn't get it out of his head. He spent every spare minute he had in the shed. He was working on what was going to be the most incredible mechanical man that had ever been made.

He made Scrapman with arms that could reach much further than an ordinary man.

He gave him telescopic legs that could stretch out as long as stilts when he needed to get to something high up.

His brain was the tricky part. Winston worked on that for weeks. He used circuits from an old TV and bits of radio pagers. He gave him the voice from a telephone answering machine.

And then he had the most tremendous piece of luck – he found the inside from an almost new Personal Organizer to use as a memory. He screwed them all together and wired them up and soldered all the connections. It wasn't a very good brain. But it was a brain.

The only thing left to do was to get Scrapman to work. For this he found an almost new car battery. He fixed it right in the middle of Scrapman and attached two jump leads.

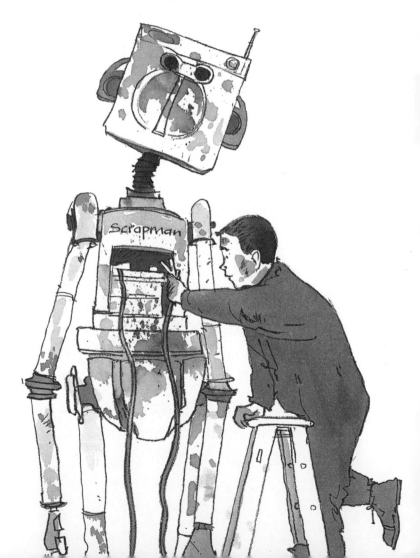

It was very late by the time
Scrapman was all wired up and ready
to start. Winston was very very tired.
He wiped his hands on an oily rag and
gazed at his wonderful mechanical
man with pride.

In the morning he was going to
come back and attach the other ends
of the jump leads to the battery in his
van. Then, he hoped and believed – if
he had done everything he should and
made all the right connections –
Scrapman would come to life!

Chapter Two

That night, while Winston was
asleep, there was the most terrible
thunderstorm. The thunder boomed
and the lightning nearly split the sky
in two. Winston was so tired he didn't
hear a thing.

But back in the shed something
amazing was happening.

ZAPP! A great jagged finger of
lightning crackled through the
window and hit Scrapman right in the
centre of his battery.

Scrapman sat bolt upright and hit
his head on the ceiling.

'Od ear,' he said. 'Ware ham I?'

And then he said: 'Hoo ham I?'

You see, the brain Winston had made for him wasn't a good brain at all.

Then Scrapman looked down and read what Winston had written on his chest – S C R A P M A N.

And then he said proudly: 'I ham Scrapman.'

He rose from the bench and stood up to his full height. His head went straight through the roof of the shed. But he didn't hurt himself because, luckily, Winston hadn't thought of giving him any nerves to feel with.

He shook himself free of the wrecked shed and strode across the scrap-yard.

'Volly od,' said Scrapman looking at the mess. 'Od ear. Od ear.'

He climbed over the corrugated iron gate and caught sight of some street lights some way up the road.

'O volly pertty,' said Scrapman and he walked up the muddy road leaving a trail of very odd footprints behind him.

The road led to a tall house which had trees and a garden around it. There was a light in a window very high up. Scrapman stretched his legs to their fullest length and looked through the window.

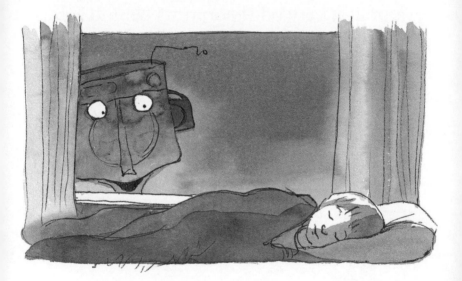

Through it, he saw a girl asleep in bed.

'A liddle gril!' said Scrapman. And he thought how clean and nice she looked fast asleep.

Then, in a flash of lightning, he caught sight of his own face reflected in the window. He saw how he was made out of old, dirty bits of machinery and he felt very ashamed of himself.

'Y ham I so ugli?' he asked himself.

He was about to tiptoe sadly away. Just then, a bolt that Winston hadn't fixed very carefully, worked its way loose in his head. It dropped with a crash on the window.

The girl, whose name was Emma,
woke up with a start.

'What was that?' she said.

And then she saw Scrapman's face
in the window.

Now any girl but Emma would have
screamed and rushed down to her
parents. But not Emma. Emma had
been waiting for quite some time for
an adventure to happen to her.

Well, it looked as if this was it!

She climbed out of bed and walked to the window.

'Hallo,' she said.

'L.O.' said Scrapman.

'Who are you?' asked Emma.

'Scrapman,' said Scrapman. 'Hoo R. U.?'

'Emma,' said Emma.

'M. R.' copied Scrapman.

'What are you doing here?' asked Emma.

Scrapman looked around him and wondered what he was doing. The thunder was still thundering and it had started raining.

'Get ting wet,' said Scrapman. And he shook himself to shake off the rain.

CREAK... GRIND... EEECH! All the joints in Scrapman's body were making dreadful screeching noises.

'Od ear,' said Scrapman.

'You poor thing. You mustn't get wet. You're getting rusty,' said Emma.

And she ran downstairs and out into the garden and opened the garage doors.

Luckily, there wasn't a car inside. Emma's parents' car had been one of the ones which had got so old and worn out and rusty, it had had to go to Winston's scrap-yard.

'Come inside quickly,' she said to Scrapman.

Scrapman almost had to fold himself in two to get into the garage. But inside it was nice and dry and he sat down thankfully on the floor.

Emma dried him off as well as she could with an old rag. Then she found an oil can and oiled his joints so that they stopped squeaking.

'O. tank U.' said Scrapman stretching his legs and arms. 'Tank U. M. R.'

Emma shook her head.

'Poor Scrapman,' she said. 'Nobody will ever understand you if you talk like that. You really must learn to talk like a human being.'

'Like a hu mung bean?' asked Scrapman.

'No,' said Emma. 'A human being.'

'Od ear,' said Scrapman.

'And it's not od ear,' said Emma.
'It's "Oh dear".'

'Oh dear,' said Scrapman carefully.
'Tank U. M. R.'

And then he tried it faster: 'Oh dear.
Oh dear. Oh dear. Od ear. Od ear.'
Then he sighed: 'Od ear.'

'Poor Scrapman,' said Emma. 'Just
keep practising until you get it right.'

She went on, 'But you can't stay here forever. Can't you remember where you've come from? Or who you belong to?'

Scrapman searched his poor brain but he couldn't remember anything.
'I dun no,' said Scrapman sadly. It's a dreadful thing not to know where you come from or who you belong to.

'Well wait here. Don't move until I come back after school,' said Emma.

'Skool?' said Scrapman. 'Wot is skool?'

'School is a big building where you go to learn things. You don't know anything do you?'

Scrapman shook his head sadly. He really did have a very poor brain.

26

Chapter Three

That morning, Winston woke up and went to his shed whistling happily to himself. Today was going to be his big day – the day when he was actually going to make his wonderful mechanical man work.

You can imagine his shock and horror when he found that the shed was empty and that there was a great gaping hole in the roof.

'Someone must have stolen him!' thought Winston. He dialled 999 straight away.

'Missing. A mechanical man about five metres high. Not seen since last night,' he told the police.

Six police cars soon arrived. Twelve policemen with their sniffer dogs climbed out.

They soon came across Scrapman's strange footprints.

Winston scratched his head. He couldn't believe his eyes.

'It looks as if he just walked away,' he said.

So the police cars set off down the road following the footprints with their sirens wailing.

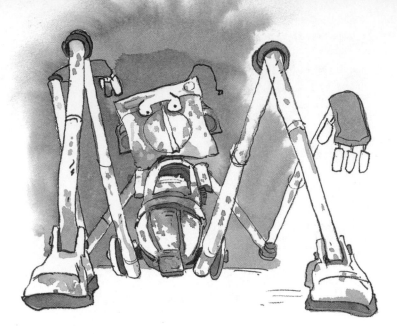

Scrapman sat in M.R.'s garage feeling bored. He wondered how long M.R. was going to be at school. He wondered what school was like. M.R. said that she went there to learn things. Maybe school was where he should go to learn to talk like a hu mung bean.

At last, he could stand it no longer. He was determined to find her. If school was such a big building, it couldn't be too hard to find.

He stood up and crashed through
the garage roof. Then he kicked aside
the doors, strode across the garden
and made off down the road. Emma's
mother ran to the window just in
time to see his great lumbering figure
disappearing around the corner.

The school wasn't far away. Scrapman could hear the sound of children's voices shouting in the playground. And as he turned the corner, sure enough, there was a really big building.

Lots of children were running around in front of it, playing games. He crossed the road to reach it and a stream of traffic screeched to a halt.

A lollipop lady dropped her lollipop and ran for it.

People on the pavement leaped for cover inside the shops. People trapped in cars and buses stared at him in horror.

'Od ear,' said Scrapman.

'Od ear. Od ear. Od ear.'

And he hurried towards the school
as fast as his big feet would carry him.

Scrapman reached the school fence
and peered over. The children stopped
playing and stared. And then one of
the smallest ones began to cry and
then all of them became frightened
and started running in all directions at
once. All, that is, apart from Emma.

She stood in the middle of the
playground and said: 'Scrapman, what
do you think you are doing here?'

Scrapman was so pleased to see her.
He climbed over the fence and
lumbered towards her.

It was at that point that Winston and Emma's mother arrived – together with the six police cars, and the twelve policemen, and the sniffer dogs, plus two fire engines that had joined in to help.

The firemen unrolled their fire hoses.

'Od ear...!' said Scrapman. He was very worried. He and M.R. were standing in the middle of the playground. The policemen, the firemen, and the sniffer dogs were moving towards them. In his poor Scrapman brain something told him that M.R. was in danger.

Scrapman could see water shooting out of the fire hoses. He didn't want M.R. to get stiff and rusty like he had.

Scrapman bent down and very gently lifted Emma off the ground. All the people gasped and the children screamed. People stood back and the police cars turned their sirens off. The crowd fell silent.

Everyone watched hardly daring to breathe as Scrapman walked over to the fire escape.

Step by step,
flight by flight, he
climbed, holding M.R. as high as he
could to keep her safe.

'Put me down, Scrapman,' cried
Emma.

'Od ear no,' said Scrapman.
'Scrapman volly good. Stop M.R.
getting wet.'

When at last he was at the top, he climbed on to the roof holding M.R. tight in his hand.

The crowd watched in horrified silence.

The chief policeman walked forward with a loud hailer.

'Put the girl down and you will not be harmed,' he bellowed.

Scrapman looked at the policeman, he looked at the fire engines, he looked at M.R. He didn't know what to do.

'Od ear,' he said.

Winston, who was watching below, pushed himself through to the front of the crowd and started to climb up the fire escape. Everyone gasped and as Winston reached the top he held up a hand for silence.

'The girl is perfectly safe,' he shouted to the crowd. 'I made Scrapman. He wouldn't harm anyone. I've come to take him back home where he belongs.'

Scrapman looked at Winston. He
looked at M.R. He couldn't believe
what he was hearing.

'He's right,' shouted Emma. 'He may
look frightening but he's kind and
gentle and...' She paused and looked
at Scrapman. 'He's a friend of mine.'

Scrapman couldn't believe that anyone could say anything so nice about him. Suddenly he didn't feel dirty and rusty any more. What did it matter if he was made out of old spare parts? Who cared?

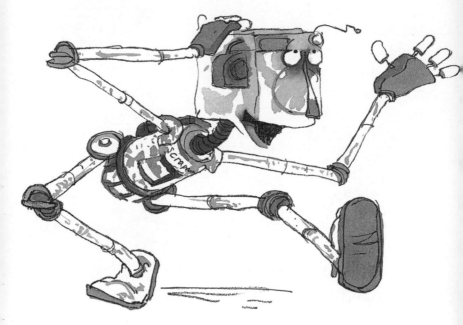

So the police and the firemen and the sniffer dogs all watched while Winston and Emma led Scrapman back to the scrap-yard.

'Od ear. Od ear,' said Scrapman when he saw the mess he had made of the shed.

But then, when he saw all the useful bits that Winston had saved inside the shed he said: 'Volly good, volly good.'

And he got busy right away sorting out some bits and pieces to mend the roof with.

In time, he turned out to be very useful indeed. He could do all the jobs that were too hard or too heavy or too high up for Winston to do.

And Emma came to give him talking lessons every Saturday.

In the end he became very good at talking indeed. He could even say really difficult things like 'automatic transmission' and 'throttle cable' and 'crankshaft' – words that came in really handy at the scrap-yard.

But when things went wrong the only thing he could ever find to say was: 'Od ear, od ear, od ear.'

About the author

I started writing in advertising, as a copywriter, scripting television commercials and writing press advertisements.

When my daughter told me that she didn't like reading, I decided to write a book for her – one that hopefully, she couldn't fail to enjoy. This was the first of many books for children. I now mainly write for teenagers under the pen-name of Chloe Rayban.

My aim in writing is to provide books that are fun to read and that can compete with the massive choice of other things on offer for young people to do.